The Arnold Book Of Old Songs

Arranged by

Roger Quilter

BOOSEY & HAWKES

AN IMAGEM COMPANY

DISTRIBUTED BY

HAL•LEONARD® CORPORATION
7777 W. BLUEMOUND RD. P.O. BOX 13819 MILWAUKEE, WI 53213

B. H. Bk. 297

To the memory of Arnold Guy Vivian

Drink to Me only with Thine Eyes

Words by
BEN JONSON (1573-1637)

English Melody
18th Century

B. & H. 15992

Printed in U.S.A.

ask a drink di - vine;............ But might I of Jove's

nec - tar sup,..... I would not change for thine.

I sent thee late a

ro - sy wreath, Not so........ much honour - ing thee,.................

Drink to Me only with Thine Eyes

B. & H. 15000

Over the Mountains

Words from
PERCY'S *Reliques*

Old English Melody

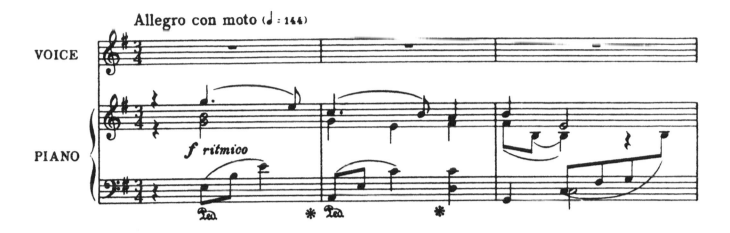

Original Key

BOOSEY & HAWKES

Un - der the...... foun - tains And...... un - der the

graves, Un - der floods.................. that are deep - est Which

Nep - tune o - bey, O - ver rocks that are

steep - est, Love will find out the way.

B. & H. 15998

Where there is...... no place For the

glow - worm to lie, Where there is...... no space For re-

- ceipt of a fly: Where the midge........ dare not ven - ture Lest her-

self fast she... lay, If....... Love come he will en - ter And will

find out the way.

Some think to..... lose him Or.... have him con-

-fined. Some do sup-pose him, Poor thing, to be

blind; But if ne'er so close ye wall him, Do the best that ye......

Over the Mountains

B. & H. 15998

may, Blind Love, if so ye call..... him, Soon will

find out his way.

You may train the eag - le To.......

stoop to your fist, Or you may in - vei - gle The

phoen - ix of the East. The...... lion - - ess you may

move her To...... get o'er her..... prey, But you'll

ne'er stop a lov - er, Love shall find out the way.................

B. & H. 15988

To the memory of Arnold Guy Vivian

My Lady Greensleeves

Words by
JOHN IRVINE

Old English Melody

but com-pare....... Nor rob....... her of........ her come - li - ness.

Come love..... be all my joy........... Thou a - lone...... art

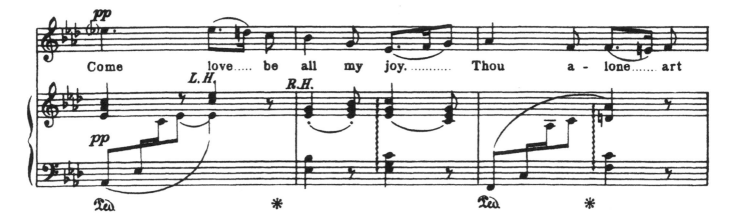

my de - light. Come love be my heart of gold..... And

who but my la - - dy Green - - sleeves.............. Oh

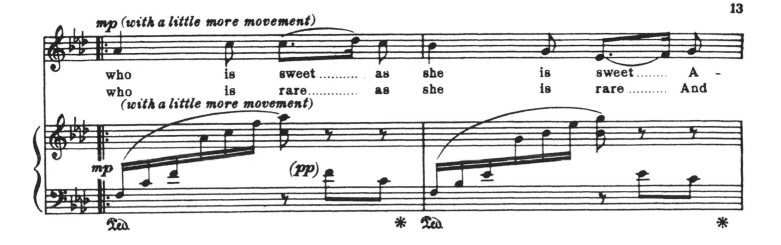

who .... is .... sweet .... as ..... she ..... is ..... sweet .... A -
who .... is .... rare .... as ..... she ..... is ..... rare .... And

- bove ..... all ..... things .... that ..... mor - - tals ..... prize: ..... I'd
who ..... is ..... such .... a ..... charm - - ing ..... maid. ..... The

lay ..... a ..... king - dom ..... at ..... her ..... feet .... Nor
lute ..... shall ..... tell ..... her ..... my ..... des - pair .... And

seek .... a ..... rich - er ..... mer - chan - dise. ..... Come ..... love .... be
fill .... with ..... song ...... the ..... myr - tle ..... shade.

My Lady Greensleeves

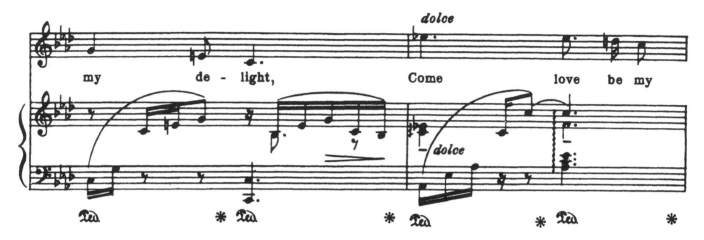

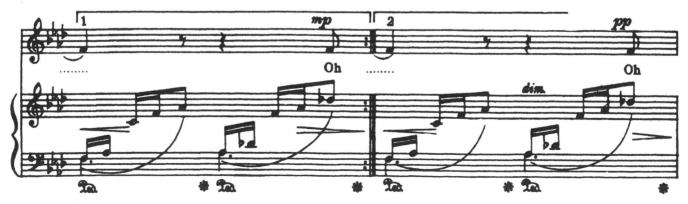

who is kind...... as she is kind......Whose gen-tle heart.... could

ne'er be-tray! If Ar - - gus prove him-self but blind....... Yet

she .... would have...... my con - stan-cy. Come love..... be

all my joy............. Thou a - lone.... art my de-light,

My Lady Greensleeves

B. & H. 18004

Believe me, if all those endearing young charms

Words by
THOMAS MOORE

Old Irish Melody

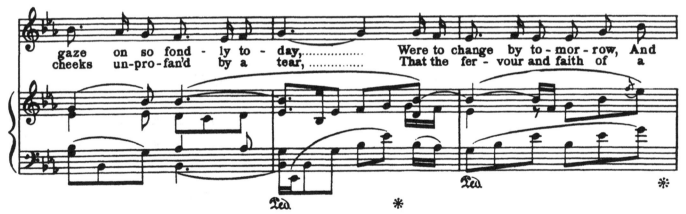

VAB-27

Printed in U.S.A.

still be a-dor'd, as this mo-ment thou art, Let thy love - li-ness fade as it
heart that has tru - ly lov'd ne - ver for-gets, But as tru - ly loves on to the

will,............. And a-round the dear ru - in each wish of my heart Would en -
close,............ As the sun - flow'r turns on her god, when he sets, The same

- twine it - self ver - dant-ly still.............
look which she turn'd when he

(2.) It.... rose................................

B. & H. 15995

Oh! 'tis sweet to think

Words by
THOMAS MOORE

Old Irish Melody

VAB-27

heart like a ten-dril, ac-cus-tom'd to cling, Let it grow where it will, can-not

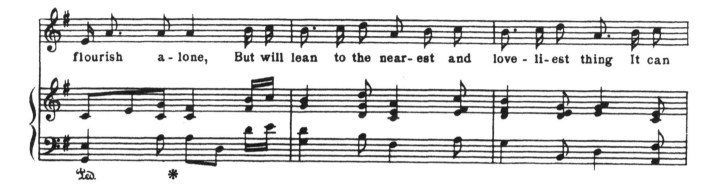

flourish a-lone, But will lean to the near-est and love-li-est thing It can

twine with it-self, And make close-ly its own. Then oh! what plea-sure, Wher-

-e'er we rove, To be doom'd to find some-thing, still, that is dear, And to

Oh! tis sweet to think

B. & H. 15996

know, when far from the lips we love, We have but to make love to the

lips we are near.

'Twere a shame, when flow-ers a -

-round us rise, To make light of the rest, If the rose is not there; And the

worlds so rich in re - splen - dent eyes, 'Twere a

pi - ty to lim - it one's love to a pair. Love's

wing and the pea - cock's are near - ly a - like; They are

both of them bright, But they're change-a-ble too: And wher-e - ver a new beam of

beau - ty can strike, It will tinc - ture love's plume with a

dif - fer-ent hue. Then oh! what plea-sure, Wher - e'er we rove, To be

doom'd to find some - thing, still, that is dear, And to know, when far from the

Strict time to end

lips we love, We have but to make love to the lips we are near.

Oh! 'tis sweet to think

B. & H. 13994

Ye banks and braes

Words by
BURNS

Old Scottish Melody

B. & H. 15997

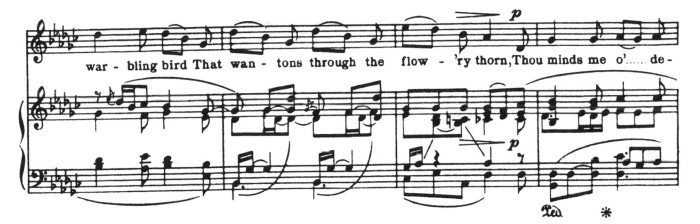

war - bling bird That wan - tons through the flow - 'ry thorn, Thou minds me o'...... de-

-part - ed joys,...... De - part - ed ne - ver to....... re - turn.

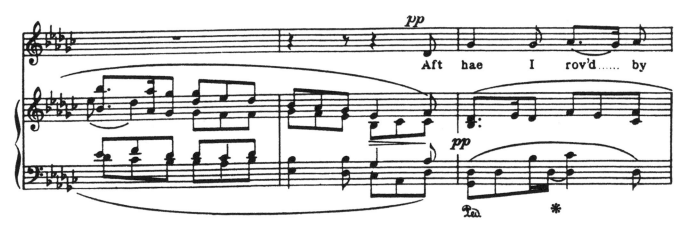

Aft hae I rov'd...... by

bon - nie Doon, To see........ the rose..... and wood - bine twine; And

Ye banks and braes

B. &

To the memory of Arnold Guy Vivian

Charlie is my darling

Words Anonymous

Scottish
Jacobite marching tune
(1775)

on a Mon - day morn - ing, Right ear - ly in the year, When

cresc.

Char - lie came to our....... town. The young.... chev - a - lier. Oh!........

mf

Char - lie is my dar - ling, my dar - ling, my dar - ling, Oh!

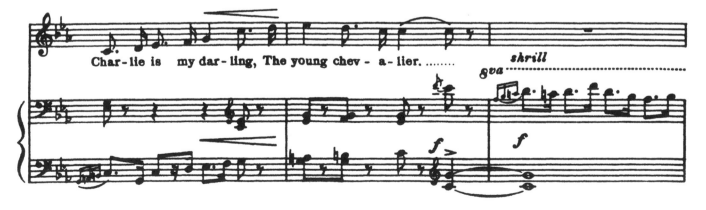

Char - lie is my dar - ling, The young chev - a - lier. ....

shrill

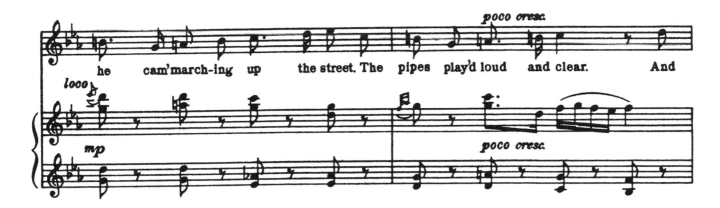

he cam' march-ing up the street. The pipes play'd loud and clear. And

a' the folk cam' rin-nin out To meet the chev-a-lier. Oh!

Char - lie is my dar - ling, my dar - ling, my dar - ling. Oh!

In time

Char - lie is my dar - ling, The young chev - a - lier.

mf

Wi' Hie - land bon - nets on their heads And

clay - mores bright and clear, They cam' to fight for Char - lie And the

young..... chev - a - lier. Oh! Char - lie is my dar - ling, my

B. & H. 15998

dar - ling, my dar - ling, Oh! Char - lie is my dar - ling, The

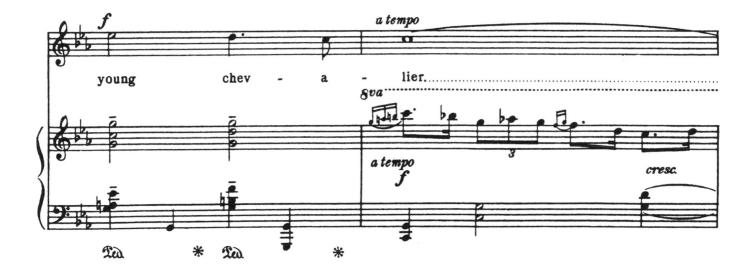

young chev - a - lier.

Charlie is my darling

To the memory of Arnold Guy Vivian

Ca' the yowes to the knowes

Words by
BURNS

Old Scottish Melody

VAB-27

Printed in U.S.A.

My bon-nie dear - ie. Hark, the ma - vis eve - ning sang,

Sound - ing Clu - den's woods a - mang; Then a fauld - ing let us gang,

My bon-nie dear - ie. Fair and love - ly as thou art,

Thou hast stol'n my ve - ry heart; I can die but can - na part,

My bon-nie dear - - ie...................

rall

a tempo
pp(far away)

Ca' the yowes

poco dim.

rall

a tempo
pp(far away)

to the knowes, Ca' them whaur the hea - ther grows,

rit - en - u - to

Ca' them where the burn - ie rows, My bon - nie dear - - ie.

rit - en - u - to

Ca' the yowes to the knowes

To the memory of Arnold Guy Vivian

The man behind the plough

Le pauvre laboureur

English Words by
RODNEY BENNETT

Old French Melody

VAB-27

Printed in U.S.A.

Come rain, ... come wind, come tem - - -
Qu'il pleuv,' .... qu'il tonn,' qu'il ven - - -

- pest, ... No mat - - ter when or how, ...
- te, ... Qu'il fas - - se mau - vais temps, ...

marcato

His toil must be un - ceas - ing, The man be - hind the
L'on voit tou - jours sans ces - se Le la - bour - eur aux
                                                    in time

plough. .... The
champs. .... Le

The man behind the plough

man be-hind.... the plough, He........ has bairns to call his own; ....
pau - vre la - bour - eur L'a .... deux pe-tits en - fants; ....

Must breed them to....... his trade, Some.... are babes and some half
Les mène à la....... char - rue, N'ont .... pas en - cor' quinze

grown. .... Come rain, ... come wind, come
ans. .... Qu'il pleuv', ... qu'il tonn', qu'il

B. & H. 16000

thun - - - der,............ No mat - - ter when or
ven - - - te,............ Qu'il fas - - se mau - vais

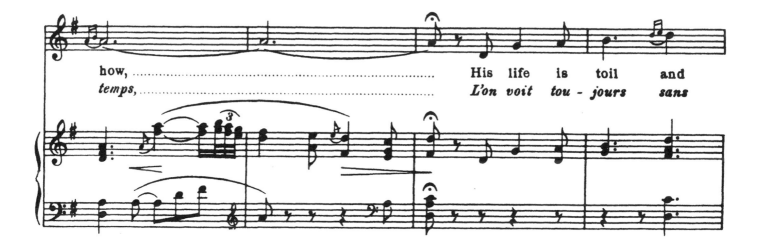

how,.. His life is toil and
temps,...................................... L'on voit tou - jours sans

la - bour, The man be - hind the plough.................... The
ces - se Le la - bour-eur aux champs.......................... Le

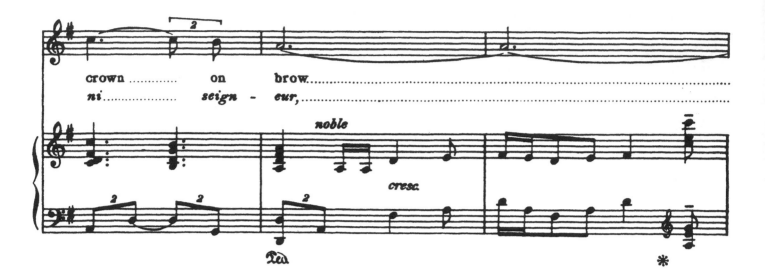

crown .... on brow..
ni............ seign - eur,..................................

.... But lives up - on his la - bour, The man be-hind....... the
.... Qui n'vi - ve de la pei - ne Du pau - vre la - bour-

plough. ....
- eur. ....

My lady's garden

L'amour de moi

English Words by
RODNEY BENNETT

Old French Melody

VAB-27

B. & H. 16001

My lady's garden

Fair - er than blos - - som red............... or white,
Je la vis l'au - - tre jour cueil - lir

Li - ly or vio - - let wet............... with dew,
La vi - o - lette en un - - vert pré.

No flow'r that blooms the sum - - mer through
La plus bel - - le qu'ono........ que je vis,

Half so fair is to............ my sight. I saw her gath-'ring
Et la plus plai - sante à mon gré. Je l'ai re - gar - dée

My lady's garden

B. & H. 16001

To the memory of Arnold Guy Vivian

Pretty month of May

Joli moi de Mai

Words Anonymous

Old French Melody

VAB-27

Printed in U.S.A.

Pretty month of May

B. & H. 16002

all my heart; We will love for e - ver, Ne - ver-
don - ne - rai; Ja - mais d'autre a - mi - e Je ne

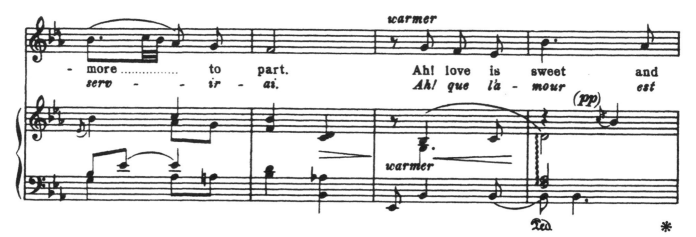

- more............... to part. Ah! love is sweet and
serv - ir - ai. Ah! que l'a - mour est

gay, The pret - ty month of May! Ah! love is sweet and
gai, Le jo - li mois de Mai! Ah! que l'a - mour est

gay, O, won - drous gay, The pret - ty month of May!........
gai, Ah! qu'il est gai, Le jo - li mois de Mai!........

The Jolly Miller

Words Anonymous

Old English Melody

Copyright 1921 by Winthrop Rogers Ltd.

BOOSEY & HAWKES

B. & H. 16008

this the bur-den of his song For ev - er used to

be............... I care for no-bod-y, no, not I, If

no - bod-y cares for me.....................

molto giocoso

I

love my mill, she is to me Both par - ent, child and

wife; .... I would not change my sta - tion for An-

-oth - er one in life. .... Then push, push, push the

bowl, my boys, And pass it round to me; .... The

The Jolly Miller

B. & H. 16008

long - er we.......... sit here and drink The mer - ri-er we shall

be. ....

Thus like the mil - ler, bold and free, Let

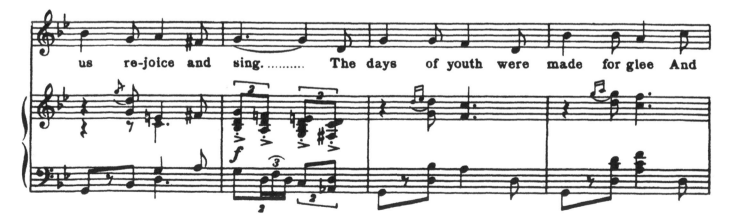

us re-joice and sing.......... The days of youth were made for glee And

time is on the wing................ This song shall pass from

me to thee A - round this jo - vial ring: .... Let

heart and voice and all a-gree To sing "Long live.... the King." ....

B. & H. 16008

Barbara Allen

Words traditional

Old English Melody

Copyright 1921 by Winthrop Rogers Ltd.

B.& H. 16004

BOOSEY & HAWKES

con

month of May When green buds they were swel-lin', Young

con

più

tristessa

Jem-my Grove on his death-bed lay For love of Bar - b'ra

tristessa

legato

sonore

Al - len. *poco appassionato* *poco dim.*

molto cresc.

Ped. *

p legato

Then slow-ly, slow - - ly she came up, And

pochiss. rit

p ben legato

B.& H. 16004

Barbara Allen

slow - ly she came nigh him, And all she said when

poco accel.

There she came "Young man, I think you're dy - ing."

mp sonoro

As

poco dim. *pochiss. rit*

she was walk - ing o'er the fields She heard the dead - bell

knel-lin', And ev-'ry stroke the...... dead-bell gave Cried

"Woe to Bar-b'ra Al-len!"

When he was dead and laid in grave Her

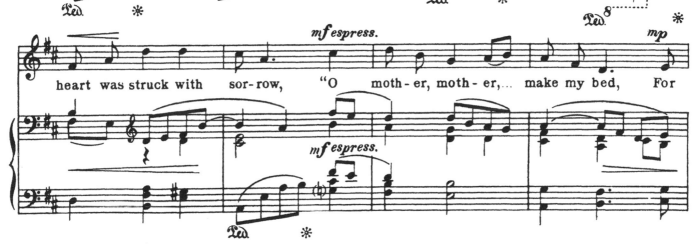

heart was struck with sor-row, "O moth-er, moth-er,... make my bed, For

I shall die to - mor - row."

"Fare-well," she said "ye vir-gins all, And shun the fault I

fell in; Hence-forth take warn-ing by the fall Of cru-el Bar - b'ra

Al - len."

B.& H. 16004

To the memory of Arnold Guy Vivian

Three Poor Mariners

Words Anonymous

Old English Melody

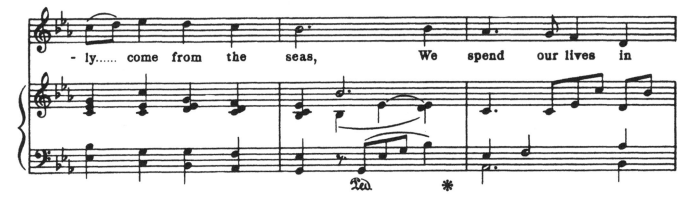

Copyright 1921 by Winthrop Rogers Ltd.

BOOSEY & HAWKES

B. & H. 16665

we'll go dance the round, the round, the round, So

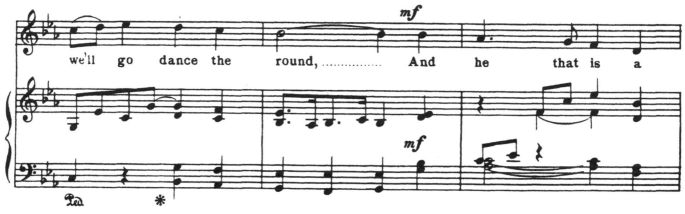

we'll go dance the round,............... And he that is a

bul-ly, bul-ly boy Come pledge me on the ground, the ground, the ground.

B. & H. 16005

Allegro a tempo Iᵐᵒ

we'll go dance the round, the round, the round, So

we'll...... go dance the round, And

he that is a bul-ly, bul-ly boy Come pledge me on the

ground, the ground, the ground, Come pledge me on the ground.........

To the memory of Arnold Guy Vivian

Since first I saw your face

Words Anonymous

Melody by
FORD
17th Century

Since first I saw your face I re-solv'd to

hon - our and re - nown you: If now I be dis -

-dain'd I........ wish my heart had ne - ver known you; What

I that lov'd and you that lik'd, Shall we be-gin to wran - gle?

No, no, no, my heart is fast And can - not dis-en - tan - gle.

If I ad-mire or praise you too much That

fault you may for - give me; Or if my hands had

stray'd to..... touch, Then just - ly might you leave me. I

ask'd you leave, you bade me love, Is't now a time to

chide me? No, no, no, I'll love you still, What for - tune e'er be -

-tide me. The sun, whose beams most glor-ious are, Re - jec - teth no be-

- hold - er, And your sweet beau-ty past com-pare made my poor eyes the

bold - er. When beau - ty moves, and wit delights, And signs of kind-ness

bind me, There, o there, where-'er I go, I'll leave my heart be - hind me.

B. & H. 16006

The Ash Grove

English words by
RODNEY BENNETT

Old Welsh Melody

see once a-gain; The voic-es of friends that the
com-ing of day! And still, spite of sor-row, when-

long years have ta-ken, Oh faint-ly I hear them, the song and the
-e'er I re-mem-ber, My thoughts will re-turn like a bird to the

word. How much in the heart can so lit-tle a-wa-ken: The
nest, No mat-ter though sum-mer may wane to De-cem-ber, And

wind in the leaves and the song of a bird! 2. How rest.
there in the Ash Grove my heart be at